W9-AZM-393

SPORTS SUPERSTARS

TODD GURLEY

By Anthony K. Hewson

Kaleidoscope
Minneapolis, MN

Your Front Row Seat to the Games

• •

This edition is co-published by agreement between Kaleidoscope and World Book, Inc.

Kaleidoscope Publishing, Inc.
6012 Blue Circle Drive
Minnetonka, MN 55343 U.S.A.

World Book, Inc.
180 North LaSalle St., Suite 900
Chicago IL 60601 U.S.A.

Kaleidoscope ISBNs
978-1-64519-049-3 (library bound)
978-1-64494-206-2 (paperback)
978-1-64519-150-6 (ebook)

World Book ISBN
978-0-7166-4353-1 (library bound)

Library of Congress Control Number
2019940068

Printed in the United States of America.

TABLE OF
CONTENTS

CHAPTER 1

Going Vertical

Todd Gurley stood in the **backfield**. He hunched over. He put his hands on his knees. Now he was ready. His Los Angeles Rams were down 20–10. They needed a big play. The ball was on the Washington 18-yard line.

The Washington defense eyed Gurley. They knew he could run and catch. They had to prepare for both.

Rams quarterback Jared Goff hands off to Todd Gurley in their game against Washington.

Gurley leaps over the Washington defense.

The play started. Gurley took off to the left. A pass was soon coming his way. Gurley pulled it in. He turned upfield. Washington **cornerback** Bashaud Breeland was in his way. Gurley had two choices. He could try to run through Breeland. Gurley had the size to do it. He was 6-foot-1 (1.85 m) and 224 pounds (102 kg). But Gurley had other ideas. He leaped into the air. Breeland dove for his legs. But Gurley soared over him. Breeland caught nothing but air.

CAREER
STATS

Through the 2018 season

RUSHING TOUCHDOWNS	46
RUSHING YARDS	4,547
RECEPTIONS	187
RECEIVING YARDS	1,883

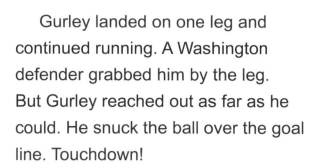

Gurley landed on one leg and continued running. A Washington defender grabbed him by the leg. But Gurley reached out as far as he could. He snuck the ball over the goal line. Touchdown!

Gurley popped up and his teammates surrounded him to celebrate. They were very familiar with his talent. He was not only a great running back. He was simply a great athlete.

FUN FACT
Todd led the NFL in rushing touchdowns in both 2017 and 2018.

Gurley stretches out for a touchdown against Washington.

CHAPTER 2

The Speedster

Todd Gurley crouched down. He placed his hands on the ground. He lifted his head. Now he was prepared to run.

Todd took off. His legs pushed him forward with every stride. An obstacle stood in his way. Todd sized it up. Then he jumped over it and landed in stride. Then Todd did it again. He wasn't jumping over football players, though. Todd was running **hurdles** in high school.

MATCHING A LEGEND

Gurley is in good company. Eric Dickerson only played four seasons for the Rams. But they were incredible ones. He became the first rookie to rush for 1,000 yards and 10 touchdowns for the Rams. Gurley matched that feat in 2015.

Todd was born August 3, 1994, in Baltimore, Maryland. But he grew up in North Carolina. He was one of the fastest athletes in the state. His coach thought he could make the Olympics one day. But Todd played many sports. He was a football and basketball star, too.

Football was not his favorite at first. Todd had played it all his life. Eventually he tired of it. Going into high school, Todd planned to focus on basketball. A coach helped him change his mind.

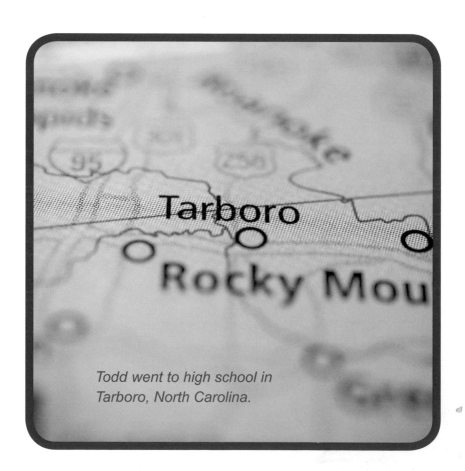

Todd went to high school in Tarboro, North Carolina.

One day, Todd was waiting for a ride home after school. Tarboro High School football coach Bo Robinson offered him one. Robinson knew about Todd. He wanted him on his team. The coach encouraged him to play.

Todd charges upfield for Tarboro High.

Where Gurley Has Been

1 **Baltimore, Maryland:** Gurley was born here.

2 **Tarboro, North Carolina:** Gurley attended high school and played football here.

3 **Athens, Georgia:** Home of the University of Georgia, where Gurley played college football.

4 **St. Louis, Missouri:** The Rams played here when Gurley started his NFL career.

5 **Los Angeles, California:** Gurley and the Rams moved here from St. Louis in 2016.

6 **Atlanta, Georgia:** Gurley played in his first career Super Bowl here after the 2018 season.

The next day, Todd showed up to practice. He dazzled with his speed. He could cut quickly and avoid defenders. But the team already had its offense set. So Todd played defense.

He got his chance at running back as a junior. His team made the state title game. Todd took a handoff. The defense was ready for him. There was no room to run. But Todd bounced off the first defender. Then another. Then another. Todd avoided six tackles in all. He ran for 46 yards to score a touchdown.

There was no doubt Todd was going on to big things. First it was at the University of Georgia. Then it was on to the NFL.

Todd scored 44 touchdowns during his three seasons at Georgia.

CHAPTER 3

Numbers for Charity

Three fans take their seats on a couch. A football game is showing on the TV. Two laptops are open, too. They are showing live stats from games all around the league. These fans are playing **fantasy football**. The winning team takes home prize money.

The Rams are playing on the TV. Todd Gurley takes the handoff. He jumps to his right. A defender flies past. Gurley scoots into the **end zone**. Touchdown, Rams!

It was yet another score for Gurley. He helped the Rams win the game. Onc of the fans cheered, too. Gurley was on that fan's fantasy team. Gurley's touchdown earned that team points, too. It also earned money for **charity**.

Gurley scored a league-high 13 rushing touchdowns in 2017.

Gurley spent time with kids at a Shriners Hospital during his college years.

Gurley never paid much attention to fantasy football. In 2017, some fantasy players were upset with him. He didn't score them enough points. Gurley tried to turn the situation into a positive. When he helped someone win, he encouraged them to donate their winnings to charity.

Fantasy players donated more than $10,000 over a few days in December 2017. Gurley was thrilled with the result.

"It doesn't matter what the money amount is—$10, $5, $25," he said. "Just to see that and people caring, that means a lot."

Most of the money went to the Shriners. Shriners build hospitals for children. Gurley has worked with the Shriners a lot. Besides raising money, he has visited sick kids in the hospital.

Gurley loves kids. He is a big kid himself. Gurley threw himself a party for his 24th birthday in 2018. Instead of a nightclub or restaurant, Gurley chose a water park.

"Water parks are just relaxing, man," he said. "You can just have fun and get on slides without fear."

Gurley and his friends rode all the slides. They had ice cream cake. And they relaxed by the pool. Gurley is intense on the field. But he loves to have fun off it.

Gurley hosts a reading and pizza party for kids in Southern California.

CAREER TIMELINE

1994

August 3, 1994
Todd Gurley is born in Baltimore, Maryland.

2011
Gurley competes in hurdles at the World Youth Championships.

2011

2012
Gurley chooses to play football at the University of Georgia.

2012

2014
Gurley decides to enter the NFL Draft after three seasons at Georgia.

2014

April 30, 2015
Gurley is drafted tenth overall by the St. Louis Rams.

2015

September 27, 2015
Gurley makes his NFL debut.

2015

2015
Gurley is named NFL Offensive Rookie of the Year and plays in his first Pro Bowl.

2015

2016
Gurley and the Rams move from St. Louis to Los Angeles.

2016

2017
Gurley is named NFL Offensive Player of the Year.

2017

2018
Gurley leads the NFL in rushing touchdowns with 17 as the Rams reach Super Bowl LIII.

2018

CHAPTER 4

LA Legend

The Rams were set up to pass. Gurley took a position wide left. That was where receivers typically line up. The Oakland Raiders thought they knew what was coming. They didn't.

Gurley suddenly sprinted to his right. Quarterback Jared Goff took the snap. In an instant, he tossed the ball forward to Gurley. Gurley outran all the tacklers. He sprinted down the sideline. He crossed the goal line and started to celebrate.

The Rams played at Los Angeles Memorial Coliseum after moving from St. Louis.

It was the team's first touchdown of the 2018 season. And the season turned out to be special. Gurley and the Rams soon reached new heights.

Gurley charges into the end zone for a touchdown against the Raiders.

In Week 13, the Rams were 10–1. They were one of the best teams in the NFL. They had a chance to clinch a **playoff** spot. But they were in a close game against the Detroit Lions.

The Rams were up by just three points in the fourth quarter. They had the ball on the Detroit 16-yard line.

Gurley roughed up the Lions in their 2018 game.

Gurley took the handoff. A few Lions were waiting. Gurley jumped to his right. He jumped to his left. There was nowhere to go. But he powered ahead for a first down. One play later, Gurley finished off the drive. He ran in for a 13-yard score.

The Lions came back to make it 23–16. The Rams wanted to put the game away. Less than three minutes remained. They faced third down from the Detroit 38-yard line. Gurley took the handoff. He stepped back and forth to fool the defense. Then he blazed ahead. One last Lion tried to tackle him and failed. The end zone was wide open.

But Gurley took a right turn. What was he doing? Instead of scoring, he ran more time off the clock. It was a smart move. He then scored two plays later.

The Rams went on to make the Super Bowl. They lost. But Gurley was coming off a great season. Rams fans looked forward to having him on the field for years to come.

Gurley evades a Patriots tackler in Super Bowl LIII.

THE BOOK

After reading the book, it's time to think about what you learned.
Try the following exercises to jumpstart your ideas.

THINK

DIFFERENT SOURCES. There are a few different types of
sources that contain information on Todd Gurley. How would each be
useful? What kind of information would a news story contain that an
encyclopedia entry might not?

CREATE

PRIMARY SOURCES. A primary source is a source that contains
firsthand information. That means it comes directly from the people who
experienced the event. What primary sources would exist that cover
Todd Gurley? Create a list of some ideas.

SHARE

WHAT'S YOUR OPINION? Chapter One states that Todd Gurley
is a great running back. Do you agree with that opinion? Find evidence
elsewhere in the book to support your position. Then share that with a
friend. Did he or she find your argument convincing?

GROW

DRAWING CONNECTIONS. How is the topic of this book connected
to other subjects you might study in school? How do Todd Gurley's
career statistics relate to math? How does a football game relate to
science? Create a diagram that shows these connections.

RESEARCH NINJA

Visit *www.ninjaresearcher.com/0493* to learn how
to take your research skills and book report writing to the next level!

RESEARCH ·

DIGITAL LITERACY TOOLS

SEARCH LIKE A PRO
Learn about how to use search engines to find useful websites.

FACT OR FAKE?
Discover how you can tell a trusted website from an untrustworthy resource.

TEXT DETECTIVE
Explore how to zero in on the information you need most.

SHOW YOUR WORK
Research responsibly—learn how to cite sources.

WRITE ·

GET TO THE POINT
Learn how to express your main ideas.

PLAN OF ATTACK
Learn prewriting exercises and create an outline.

DOWNLOADABLE REPORT FORMS

29

Further Resources

BOOKS

Bankston, John. *Jared Goff*. Mitchell Lane Publishers, 2018.

Lajiness, Katie. *Los Angeles Rams*. Abdo Publishing, 2017.

McGee, Earl. *Los Angeles Rams*. Abdo Publishing, 2017.

WEBSITES

FACTSURFER

Factsurfer.com gives you a safe, fun way to find more information.

1. Go to www.factsurfer.com.

2. Enter "Todd Gurley" into the search box and click Q.

3. Select your book cover to see a list of related websites.

Glossary

backfield: The backfield is the area behind the offensive line of a football team. Gurley stood in the backfield before the play.

charity: A charity is an organization that helps people in need. Gurley works with charities such as Shriners hospitals.

cornerback: A cornerback is a defensive football player who usually covers wide receivers. Gurley jumped over the Washington cornerback to score a touchdown.

end zone: The end zone is a 10-yard long (or deep) area where touchdowns are scored. Gurley caught a pass in the end zone for a score.

fantasy football: Fantasy football is a game in which players win or lose based on the performance of real football players. Gurley's two-touchdown game helped fantasy football players win.

hurdles: Hurdles are an event in track and field in which runners race while jumping over obstacles. Gurley ran hurdles in high school.

playoffs: The playoffs are the games among the best teams in a league and determine the champion. Gurley led the Rams to the playoffs.

rookie: A rookie is an athlete in his or her first year in a new league. Gurley matched Eric Dickerson's great success as a rookie.

Index

PHOTO CREDITS

The images in this book are reproduced through the courtesy of: Tom DiPace/AP Images, front cover (center); Mark J. Terrill/AP Images, front cover (right); Ryan Kang/AP Images, pp. 3, 17, 26–27; Jeff Bukowski/Shutterstock Images, p. 4; NFL Photos/AP Images, p. 5; Matt Patterson/AP Images, pp. 6, 8–9; Red Line Editorial, p. 7 (chart), 14, 21 (timeline); Jae C. Hong/AP Images, p. 7 (Todd Gurley); sirtravelalot/Shutterstock Images, p. 11; atdr/Shutterstock Images, p. 12; Alan Campbell/Rocky Mount Telegram/AP Images, p. 13; Cecil Copeland/Cal Sport Media/AP Images, p. 15; gpointstudio/Shutterstock Images, p. 16; Rich Graessle/Icon Sportswire/AP Images, p. 18; David Lee/Shutterstock Images, p. 19; Casey Rodgers/Pizza Hut/AP Images, p. 20; Mtsaride/Shutterstock Images, pp. 21 (football), 30; Eric Broder Van Dyke/Shutterstock Images, p. 22; Ben Margot/AP Images, p. 23; Rey Del Rio/AP Images, pp. 24–25.

ABOUT THE AUTHOR

Anthony K. Hewson is a freelance writer originally from San Diego, now living in the Bay Area with his wife and their two dogs.